WORLD'S BIGGEST

BIRDS

by Mari Schuh

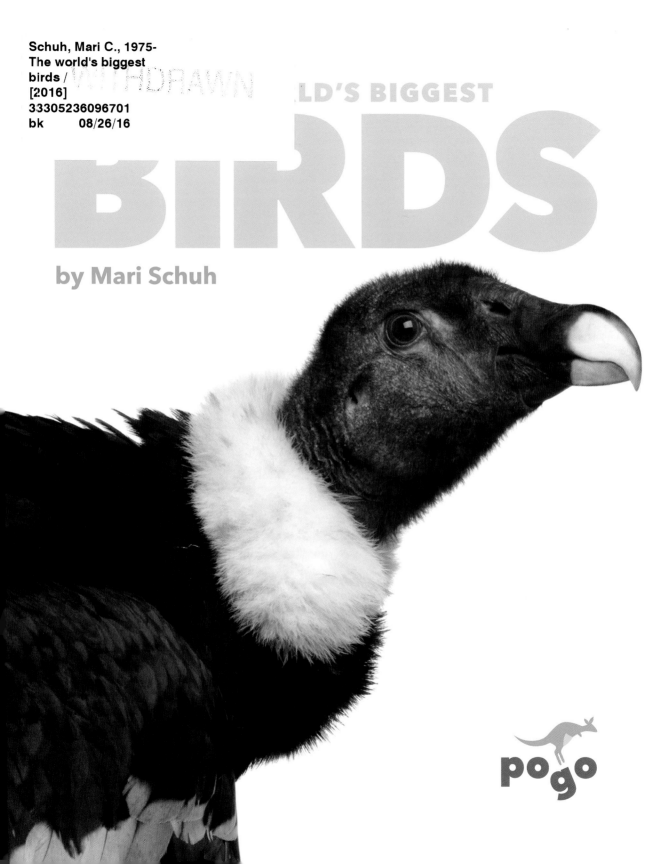

pogo

Ideas for Parents and Teachers

Pogo Books let children practice reading informational text while introducing them to nonfiction features such as headings, labels, sidebars, maps, and diagrams, as well as a table of contents, glossary, and index.

Carefully leveled text with a strong photo match offers early fluent readers the support they need to succeed.

Before Reading

- "Walk" through the book and point out the various nonfiction features. Ask the student what purpose each feature serves.
- Look at the glossary together. Read and discuss the words.

Read the Book

- Have the child read the book independently.
- Invite him or her to list questions that arise from reading.

After Reading

- Discuss the child's questions. Talk about how he or she might find answers to those questions.
- Prompt the child to think more. Ask: What is the biggest bird you have ever seen?

Pogo Books are published by Jump!
5357 Penn Avenue South
Minneapolis, MN 55419
www.jumplibrary.com

Library of Congress Cataloging-in-Publication Data

Schuh, Mari C., 1975- author.
   The world's biggest birds / by Mari Schuh.
      pages cm. – (The world's biggest animals)
   Audience: Ages 7-10
   Includes index.
   ISBN 978-1-62031-206-3 (hardcover: alk. paper) –
   ISBN 978-1-62031-261-2 (paperback) –
   ISBN 978-1-62496-293-6 (ebook)
   1. Birds–Size–Juvenile literature.
   2. Birds–Juvenile literature. I. Title.
   QL676.2.S384 2016
   598–dc23
                                           2014048939

Series Editor: Jenny Fretland VanVoorst
Series Designer: Anna Peterson
Photo Researcher: Anna Peterson

Photo Credits: All photos by Shutterstock except: age fotostock, 8-9, 10-11; Dreamstime, 14; Nature Picture Library, 20-21; SuperStock, 5, 16-17; Thinkstock, cover, 15, 18-19.

Printed in the United States of America at Corporate Graphics in North Mankato, Minnesota.

TABLE OF CONTENTS

CHAPTER 1

WHAT ARE BIRDS?

A bald eagle **soars** in the sky.

A penguin swims in the **ocean**.

What do these animals have in common?

They are both **birds**. Birds have feathers and wings. They lay eggs. Most birds fly. But some cannot.

CHAPTER 2

HIGH IN THE SKY

Andean condors are one of the biggest flying birds.

They can weigh up to 33 pounds (15 kilograms). That is more than a two-year-old child!

Andean condors have huge wings. They have the biggest wing area of any bird.

Their wings are both wide and deep.

Andean condors often fly in windy areas. The wind helps them soar a long way.

DID YOU KNOW?

An Andean condor's wings can be 10 feet (3 meters) wide. That is wider than a car!

width ┄┄┄▶

depth

Andean condors are **vultures**.

They feast on dead sheep and cattle. They also eat dead fish, seals, and even whales.

Andean condors can fly more than 100 miles (161 kilometers) in a day looking for dead animals.

DID YOU KNOW?

Andean condors can fly 18,000 feet (5,486 m) in the air. That's more than three miles (4.8 km)! They flap their wings only once an hour.

Andean condors can eat more than four pounds (1.8 kg) of meat at one time.

These hungry birds get so full that they cannot fly. They rest on land until they can fly again.

WHERE ARE THEY?

Andean condors live in the mountains and deserts of South America. They live near the **coast**.

SOUTH AMERICA

■ = Andean Condor Range

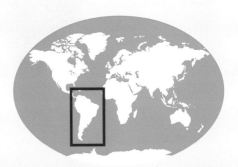

BIG BIRDS

Ostriches are the biggest birds in the world.

They can weigh up to 350 pounds (159 kg).

Ostriches are also the tallest birds. Some are nine feet (2.7 m) tall.

That is much taller than a human adult.

large ostrich

average human

These birds are so big that they cannot fly at all. But they can run.

Their long legs can cover more than 10 feet (3 m) in just one stride.

Ostriches can sprint up to 45 miles (72 km) an hour.

That is faster than most birds can fly!

DID YOU KNOW?

Ostriches have the biggest eyes of any land animal. Each eye is two inches (5 centimeters) across. That's bigger than the bird's brain!

Ostriches use their long, strong legs to stay safe.

They hurt **predators** with a powerful kick.

Their long toes and thick nails hurt predators, too.

DID YOU KNOW?

Ostriches lay the world's biggest eggs. One egg weighs about three pounds (1.4 kilograms.) That is as much as 24 chicken eggs.

WHERE ARE THEY?

Ostriches live in Africa's deserts and grassy plains. They often live together in small **flocks**.

AFRICA

■ = Ostrich Range

Huge birds soar high in the sky. Birds run on land and swim in oceans, too.

What is the biggest bird you have ever seen?

ACTIVITIES & TOOLS

HOW TALL?

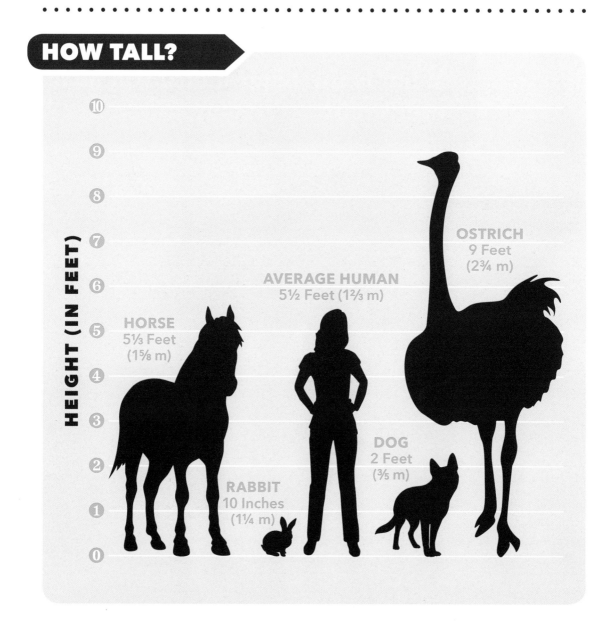

HEIGHT (IN FEET)

10
9
8
7
6
5
4
3
2
1
0

OSTRICH
9 Feet
(2¾ m)

AVERAGE HUMAN
5½ Feet (1⅔ m)

HORSE
5⅓ Feet
(1⅝ m)

DOG
2 Feet
(⅗ m)

RABBIT
10 Inches
(1¼ m)

TRY THIS!

Andean condors' wings can stretch 10 feet (3 m) wide.
How far can you stretch?

1. **Stand and then spread your arms out wide.**

2. **Have an adult measure your arms using a tape measure.**

3. **How wide was your reach?**

. . . .

GLOSSARY

bird: An animal that has feathers and wings and can lay eggs; most birds can fly.

coast: The land next to or near an ocean or sea.

flock: A group of animals that live together.

mate: The male or female partner of a pair of animals.

ocean: A large body of salt water.

predator: An animal that hunts other animals for food.

soar: To fly or glide high in the air.

vulture: A large bird that eats dead animals.

INDEX

TO LEARN MORE

Learning more is as easy as 1, 2, 3.

1) Go to www.factsurfer.com

2) Enter "biggestbirds" into the search box.

3) Click the "Surf" to see a list of websites.

With factsurfer, finding more information is just a click away.